Allie's First Ballet Exam

Judy John-Baptiste

This book belongs to:

_____ isabella clark _____

_____

Today is a very important day for Allie. Today she has her first ballet exam. She is very excited.

Allie has a new pair of pink tights, and a hair net which her mum will neatly fasten with hair pins. Her skirted leotard smells like fresh flowers and her ballet slippers are sitting in her bag.

As Allie starts to get dressed she remembers Miss Hope her ballet teacher
telling her,

*Don't forget to point your toes! Don't forget to smile
at the examiner.*

Allie always tried her best to smile in class but sometimes she forgot.

She pointed her toes most of the time, but sometimes she forgot that

too.

All Allie's friends go to the dance studio. They all love ballet. They are best friends. Emma, Lisa, Olive and Nadia are all taking their first ballet exam. Today is an important day for everyone!

When Allie arrives at the studio she looks everywhere for Miss Hope her ballet teacher. *But where is Miss Hope today?* Allie can't find Miss Hope anywhere. Allie walks to the ballet studio to see if she is there.

The ballet studio looks different. It is very quiet. The mirrors are covered with thick black curtains. Nobody is around except a lady sitting at a large table reading. *That must be the examiner,* Allie says to herself. That must be Miss Sharp. Ooh! Allie's tummy starts to feel a little strange. The examiner looks very serious.

Allie quickly walks to the changing room to see if Miss Hope is there. But no, she is not there. Happily Allie finds all of her friends. Emma, Lisa, Olive and Nadia are all in the changing room. They are sitting with their mummies waiting for the ballet exam to start.

Allie is relieved to see all of her friends. Everyone is excited. They are all talking about the ballet exam.

The girls have been working extra hard in their ballet lessons. They have listened to everything Miss Hope has told them. They have all learned their steps. They have learned to plié, degagé, sauté and skip. They can now perform port de bras beautifully. Miss Hope has taught them well. They are perfectly prepared for their first exam.

They can all point their toes and smile.

Miss Hope jauntily walks into the changing room.

"Girls, are we ready to go?"

"Yes Miss Hope," the girls all nod nervously.

"When you go into the studio don't forget to say good morning to Miss Sharp," says Miss Hope. "She is waiting for you in the studio".

"Yes Miss Hope," the girls reply.

Allie and the girls timidly follow Miss Hope out of the changing room.

Allie feels very strange. She has never felt like this before.

She has butterflies fluttering around in her tummy!

The children walk into the studio. Miss Sharp is sitting upright.

"Good morning Miss Sharp," say the girls timidly.

Miss Sharp looks up and peers at all the children one by one. She does not respond. They all have number cards pinned onto their leotards.

Miss Sharp looks at their number cards and starts to write on the paper in front of her.

"Good morning children," she says. "Please take your position at the barre so we may begin."

Allie and the girls walk slowly to the barre.

The butterflies are dancing around in Allie's tummy.

She has forgotten to smile.

The music begins and all the girls start to demi plié. They bend and stretch gracefully in time to the music. Allie is in the middle of the barre; Emma is in front of her and Olive is behind her. She is nervous but it feels good to know she is not alone.

Suddenly Miss Sharpe says,

"Thank you children. Please come forward, I would like to see port de bras."

Port de bras? Allie has forgotten what port de bras is. The butterflies are leaping around in her tummy and she struggles to think clearly. She peers across to Emma and then looks at Olive. They are happily smiling at the examiner.

The music starts. It is very familiar to Allie. Miss Hope plays this song in every lesson. Thankfully Allie remembers port de bras just in time. She dances beautifully and so do all of the girls . Everybody is smiling except poor Allie . This ballet exam is harder than she expected!

When they have finished, the girls move quickly to form a circle in the centre of the studio.. Allie is confused.

What is happening? Why can't I remember? she asks herself.

"Err number four can you please move into position," says
Miss Sharp looking rather cross.

But Allie does not move. She stands as still as a statue. Miss Sharp stares angrily at Allie hoping this will prompt her to move.

Allie slowly shuffles into line. She starts to panic. She cannot remember what the next ballet step is.

What comes next? she asks herself. She tries hard to remember. Poor Allie does not feel at all well.

The music starts. Emma, Lisa, Olive and Nadia start skipping happily in a circle. Allie does not move an inch. All the girls skip past her.

They all wonder why Allie isn't skipping.

" Can we stop the music please!" shouts Miss Sharp.

The music stops and all the girls stop skipping abruptly.

Everyone is looking at Allie.

"Number four, can you please start skipping with the rest of the girls. If you don't, you will not pass your exam today!"

Allie begins to feel the tears welling up in her eyes. She looks over to the studio door and is tempted to run out . But to leave without finishing the exam would be terrible! *I have worked so hard preparing for today. What would Miss Hope say? Why can't I remember things today?*

Think Allie, think, she tells herself.

The butterflies are galloping around in her tummy.

"Music please," says Miss Sharp.

The girls form a circle once more. The music starts again.

Allie hears the music. She knows the song. She tries to forget she is in an exam and the examiner is watching her. She knows she has to skip.

Skip Allie! Come on you can do it, she tells herself. Her skips are heavy and very small. She barely gets off the floor, but at least she is skipping. Slowly her skips get bigger and bigger. Before long she is skipping normally. She is finally skipping with the rest of the girls in a circle!

What a relief!

"At last!" shouts the examiner.

The girls are overjoyed; Allie is skipping!

The exam is almost finished.

The girls return to the changing rooms.

"What happened Allie?" asks Emma. Emma had never seen Allie struggle in class before. It was quite a surprise.

" I don't know," says Allie almost near to tears. "I couldn't remember what to do and my tummy was hurting".

Miss Hope enters jauntily into the changing room and happily announces, " Well done girls, I think you all performed really well in your first ballet exam."

"Miss, do you think Allie did well?" asks Nadia.

"I think so," assures Miss Hope.

"But Miss, Allie didn't want to skip" says Nadia.

"I think Allie had something called stage fright. It is when you have to perform and you forget what you have to do. Sometimes you can't think clearly and you get butterflies in your tummy. When you have stage fright everything seems so much harder to do. It can happen to anybody. Luckily it doesn't last forever. Well done Allie, I think you managed your stage fright very well indeed."

Allie listened carefully to everything Miss Hope said. She
thought for a moment. *Yes I think I had stage fright.*
She now understood why everything seemed so difficult. Allie
was suffering from stage fright. Allie felt so much better now
that she had an explanation for her odd behaviour. She had
never forgotten her ballet steps before with Miss Hope.

Several weeks later Miss hope arrives in the studio with her
arms brimming over with documents . She is carrying a file
full of ballet certificates.
" Well done girls! You have all passed your first
ballet exam. I knew you all would. The first exam is always
the hardest. I'm so proud of you all."

She gives each of them their first ballet certificate. The girls are very happy and are beaming with pride. Allie remembers the exam and her first experience of stage fright. She remembers the butterflies fluttering in her tummy. It was hard to smile and she couldn't remember her steps. Yes, she agrees with Miss Hope, her first ballet exam was hard.

"Now we have passed the first exam, we now have the second to think about. Who would like to take the next ballet exam?" Without any hesitation the children's hands shoot up into the air. Allie's hands go up too. Everybody is smiling. Allie is smiling too.

Allie has the biggest smile of them all!

For more books please go to the site:
www.teachingballetcreatively.com

Printed in Great Britain
by Amazon